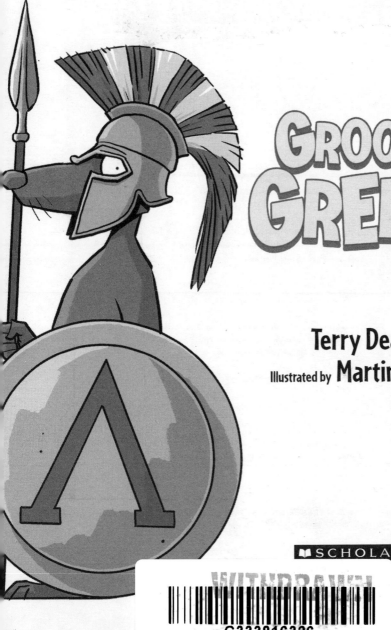

GROOVY GREEKS

Terry Deary

Illustrated by **Martin Brown**

■SCHOLASTIC

For Jean Longstaff, with thanks

Scholastic Children's Books,
Euston House, 24 Eversholt Street,
London NW1 1DB, UK

A division of Scholastic Ltd
London ~ New York ~ Toronto ~ Sydney ~ Auckland
Mexico City ~ New Delhi ~ Hong Kong

First published in the UK by Scholastic Ltd, 1996
This abridged edition published by Scholastic Ltd, 2014

Text copyright © Terry Deary, 1996, 2014
Illustrations copyright © Martin Brown, 1996, 2014
Index by Caroline Hamilton

Some of the material in this book has previously been published in Horrible Histories: Awesome Ancient Quiz Book

ISBN 978 1407 13582 3

Printed and bound by CPI Group (UK) Ltd, Croydon, CR0 4YY

2 4 6 8 10 9 7 5 3

The right of Terry Deary and Martin Brown to be identified as the author and illustrator of this work respectively has been asserted by them in accordance with the Copyright, Designs and Patents Act, 1988.

Contents

Introduction

History can be horrible. And do you know who to blame?

ER... MR POPPLECRUMP, MY HISTORY TEACHER?

No, it's the Greeks!

BUT THE ANCIENT GREEKS ARE DEAD AREN'T THEY?

DUNNO. WAS IT IN THE NEWSPAPERS?

The Greeks invented history about 2,500 years ago...

Inventing history is just one of the things we have to thank them for. They had the idea for plays, for the Olympic Games – even the camera...

Funny you should mention that. Here is a book on the groovy Greeks. A book that will tell you all the things that teacher doesn't tell you. The things you really want to know. The hilarious stories and the horror stories.

Groovy Greek Timeline

BC
1600–1200

First Greek civilizations, ruled by the mighty Mycenaean lords of Crete.

About 1180

The siege of **Troy** – Troy loses to the famous wooden horse trick.

About 1100

The state of Sparta starts.

776

First recorded Olympic games.

About 750–550

Greeks take to the seas and become great traders.

About 730

Greeks produce the first works of written poetry in the world. Groovy **Homer** is the most famous.

640

World's first roof tiles manufactured at Temple of Hera at Olympia.

About 600

Thales, the Greek scientist, announces that the entire earth is actually floating in water.

585

Scientist Thales predicts an eclipse of the sun.

About 550

First plays performed. King **Croesus** of Lydia has gold and silver coins made; the first coins with writing on them.

About 530

Peisistratus of Athens creates a library.

About 520

Alcmaeon of Croton finds out about the human body by cutting up dead ones – groovy, eh?

490

Persians invade Greece – beaten by Greeks at the Battle of **Marathon**.

486

The first comedy drama at Athens.

480

Xerxes of Persia attacks the Greeks. The battle of Thermopylae. Spartan heroes die.

460

Athens v Sparta and Persia.

431–404

Athens tries to get too bossy so the others fight the **Peloponnesian** War. Sparta becomes top dog.

430

Great Plague of Athens kills Athenian leader, **Pericles**, not to mention a quarter of all the Athenian people.

413

A defeat at Syracuse for the army of Athens followed by...

404

The Fall of Athens.

About 400

Greek army engineers invent the stomach bow – the first type of crossbow.

371

Spartans lose to new top dog, the Thebans.

336

Alexander the Great becomes King of Macedon when his dad is assassinated. In just ten years he conquers the old enemy, Persia.

330

Aristotle invents the 'camera obscura' – a sort of pinhole camera and the idea behind today's film and television – now that really was groovy!

323

Alexander the Great dies. His generals divide up his empire.

322

The end of democracy in Athens when the Macedons take over.

215

Archimedes invents war machines like the catapult – they keep the Romans out for three years.

213

Archimedes has mirrors set along the harbour walls – they dazzle the Romans and set fire to their boats ... Romans delayed for a while but...

212

Here come the **Romans**.

146

Greece part of the Roman Empire.

AD 393

Romans abandon Olympic Games – they don't happen again for 1,500 years.

Fight Like a Greek

The wooden heads of Troy

Everybody knows the story of the wooden horse of Troy.

But can you believe it? Those Trojan twits saw a wooden horse standing outside the gates of the city…

THAT'S KIND OF THEM. THEY SPEND TEN YEARS TRYING TO MURDER US THEN GO OFF AND LEAVE US A PRESENT...

JUST TO SHOW THERE'S NO HARD FEELINGS, I SUPPOSE

IT'LL LOOK VERY NICE THERE OUTSIDE THE WALLS

I'VE GOT A GREAT IDEA. WHY DON'T WE BRING IT *INSIDE* THE CITY. WE CAN HAVE IT AS A SORT OF STATUE IN THE CENTRE OF THE CITY

NOT A LOT OF WOODEN STATUES ABOUT

WE'LL BE THE FIRST. START A NEW FASHION

Everyone thinks it's a wonderful story. No one stops to ask, 'Would the Trojans really be that stupid?' But, if they *did* ask that question, the answer would have to be 'Yes.' If brains were gunpowder the Trojans wouldn't have had enough to blow their helmets off. Because they were tricked into letting the groovy Greeks into their city a *second* time.

That's right. Everyone knows about the wooden horse trick. Teachers forget to tell you about the *second* one over 800 years later in 360 BC...

Tricking a Trojan ... again

Charidemus was fed up. He paced up and down in his tent and rubbed a strong hand through his greying hair. He complained, 'I'll never capture Troy. The walls are just too strong ... and the Trojans don't look as if they're starving to death, do they?'

'No, sir,' his young lieutenant mumbled. 'Perhaps if we made a wooden horse and…'

Charidemus glared at him. 'Thank you. You are the fiftieth person to suggest that. The Trojans won't fall for that old trick again. Next time they'll just set fire to the wooden horse. Would you like to volunteer to sit inside it, eh? See if I'm right?'

The young man turned red and said, 'No, sir.'

He was relieved to hear someone approaching the tent. He jumped to the door.

'Password?'

'Ajax,' the man called.

The lieutenant opened the flap and said, 'Enter, friend.'

The guard stepped through, pulled on a short chain and dragged a ragged man through after him. The guard stood to attention. 'Spy, sir. Caught him stealing food. Permission to execute him, sir?' he barked.

General Charidemus peered at the prisoner. The man's clothes were dusty but quite rich. 'Not yet, Captain. Leave us together.'

The guard saluted and strode out. Charidemus nodded to a cushion. 'Sit down,' he ordered. 'Your name?'

The prisoner grinned. 'Damon.' He was a wiry man with dark eyes that seemed to dart around and couldn't meet anyone else's gaze.

'And you've come out from Troy to steal our food? Are things that bad inside the city then?'

Damon smiled slyly. 'You Greeks eat better than the Trojans. Even before the siege the king gave us poor rations.'

'You don't like the king? Then why work for him?' the Greek general asked.

The prisoner shrugged. 'It's a job.'

Charidemus leaned forward. 'And if I offered you a job? A better paid and better fed job?'

Damon looked at his thumb and slowly placed it in his mouth. 'I'd be happy to work for you. I'd be loyal to you.'

The general's eyes were hard as iron as he replied, 'Oh, you'd be loyal, Damon. Men who betray me die … but they die very slowly.'

The prisoner squirmed on his cushion and gave a nervous smile. 'What do you want me to do?'

'I want you to be my wooden horse, Damon. Listen carefully and I'll tell you exactly what I want you to do…'

It took a week for Charidemus to prepare the plan. His young lieutenant was nervous. As he tightened the buckle on his general's armour he asked, 'How do you know Damon won't betray us?'

The general tested the weight of his short sword. 'Damon is greedy but he's not stupid. He knows that we will take Troy sooner or later. If we have to wait too long to get inside he knows we'll be angry. We'll certainly kill the Trojan men – including him. But if he helps us he lives – and doesn't have to go to bed hungry any more.'

Charidemus slid the sword into his belt. 'Pass me my cloak.'

The young man took the large, filthy cloak and slid it over his general's wide shoulders. A hood covered the man's square head. He arranged the cloak to cover the weapons, dusted his hands and gave a nod. 'You'll pass as a poor traveller, sir.' The lieutenant changed too.

The general strode out of his tent and met a dozen men dressed the same way. No one spoke. Charidemus led the way from the torch-lit camp on to the stony road to Troy. A small man sat quietly on a horse and watched them approach.

'Is everything ready, Damon?' the general asked softly.

'It is,' the small man smiled. He turned his horse and walked slowly back towards the city gates. The Greek soldiers dragged their sandals and began to limp towards the enemy city.

'Who goes there?' a guard cried from a gate tower.

'Damon!' the traitor cried.

'Ah, so it is! What have you got with you?'

'The Greeks are growing careless. I went to their camp and found some of our captured men with just a single guard. I killed him and brought them back,' Damon lied. 'But let me in quickly. They're weak and sick!'

'Aye, Damon ... oh, you'd better give the password.'

'Castor,' Damon said quickly.

The gates creaked slowly open. The man on the horse rode in – the soldiers trudged behind him.

As the gates closed the men stood in the shadow of the wall and shrugged off their cloaks. They climbed the stone stairways to the gate towers and the walls.

The Trojan defenders had no chance. They were looking for Greeks outside the walls – they didn't expect the attack to come from within.

Charidemus cut the throat of the last guard and let the limp body drop into the dark and dusty ditch that ran outside the wall. The Greeks gathered in the tower above the gate.

'Now we wait for the rest of our army…' the general began, but his lieutenant hurried to the walls and looked over. There was a rattle of stones on the road as a body of armed men arrived and halted.

'They're here, sir, but they're too early!' the young man gasped.

'Either that or they aren't *our* men,' Charidemus said.

'How can we tell in the darkness?'

'The password, man, the password … you know, "Wooden Horse". Quick! Challenge them,' the general ordered.

'Who goes there?' the lieutenant called.

'Friend!' came the reply.

'Give the password.'

After a moment a voice called, 'Castor!'

The Greeks looked at General Charidemus. 'Let them in. If we don't they'll raise the alarm before our men get here. Hide behind the gates. As soon as the last man is in, you come out. Kill them. Kill every last one!'

The Greeks trotted down the stairs to their positions while the general and his lieutenant turned the winches that opened the gates. There was the sound of marching feet, cries of surprise and fear, the clash of weapons, then the silence of death.

From the darkest shadow of the Trojan street a small man gave a grim smile as he sat astride his horse. A horse that had led the enemy into Troy … again.

The truth about Troy

But was the story of Troy a 'history' story? Did it really happen? Homer was writing hundreds of years after the event. Of course, the story could have been passed down by word of mouth through the Dark Ages. Ask a historian...

WAS THERE A PLACE CALLED TROY?

YES. ARCHAEOLOGISTS HAVE FOUND THE SITE OF THE RUINS

•TROY

TURKEY

RUINS? SO WAS IT DESTROYED BY WAR?

IT WAS DESTROYED AND REBUILT SEVERAL TIMES ONCE IT WAS DESTROYED BY AN EARTHQUAKE

DID HELEN OF TROY REALLY EXIST?

DON'T KNOW. BUT IT WASN'T UNUSUAL FOR RAIDERS TO CARRY OFF QUEENS. SHE *COULD* HAVE EXISTED

AND WHAT ABOUT THE SACRIFICE OF IPHIGENIA?

POSSIBLE. THERE WERE CERTAINLY CASES OF CHILDREN BEING SACRIFICED - AND EVEN PARTLY EATEN - IN THOSE DAYS

YEUCH! WHAT ABOUT THE WOODEN HORSE?

INTERESTING, THAT ONE, IT COULD HAVE BEEN A POETIC IDEA FOR A WOODEN BATTERING-RAM

... IT WOULD HAVE HAD A COVER TO KEEP THE DEFENDERS' ARROWS OFF THE ATTACKERS. THE COVER COULD HAVE BEEN HORSE-SHAPED

THEN THERE'S ANOTHER INTERESTING BUT CRAZY THEORY...

WHAT'S THAT?

REMEMBER THE EARTHQUAKE? SUPPOSE THE GREEK ATTACKERS COULDN'T GET INTO TROY. AND SUPPOSE AN EARTHQUAKE CRACKED THE WALLS AND LET THEM IN...

CRACK!

Don't tell tales

As well as plays, the ancient Greeks liked a good story. And nobody told better stories than Aesop. They are still popular today. Everybody's heard of *The Tortoise and the Hare*. The moral of that story is, 'Slow and steady wins the race'. Or *The Boy who Cried Wolf*, the moral of this story being, 'No one believes a liar – even if they start telling the truth.'

He gave us wise proverbs like, 'Never count your chickens before they're hatched'. But the most terrible tale of all is about Aesop himself.

Aesop was a Greek folk hero who is supposed to have lived in the 6th century BC. One legend says he was born in Thrace, lived for a while as a slave on Sámos Island, was set free and travelled round the other states telling his stories.

Then he arrived at Delphi where the Oracle was. In ancient Greece, a priest or priestess who passed on advice from the gods was called an Oracle. Aesop seems to have upset the priests of the Oracle. Maybe he told the story of…

The man and the wooden god

In the old days, men used to worship sticks and stones and idols, and prayed to them to give them luck. It happened that a man had often prayed to a wooden idol he had received from his father, but his luck never seemed to change. He prayed and he prayed, but still he remained as unlucky as ever.

One day in the greatest rage he went to the wooden god, and with one blow swept it down from its stand. The idol broke in two, and what did he see? An immense number of coins flying all over the place.

And the moral of the story is, 'Religion is just a con trick created to make money for the priests.'

Whatever Aesop said, the priests didn't like it one little bit. They took him to the top of a cliff and threw him down to his death.

The Savage Spartans

The first great state to grow after the Dark Ages was Sparta. The Spartan people were a bit odd. They believed they were better than anyone else. If the Spartans wanted more land then they just moved into someone else's patch. If someone was already living there the Spartans just made them slaves. In short, they were the ungrooviest lot in the whole of Greece.

YOU HAVE A CHOICE, GIVE UP ALL YOUR LAND AND POSSESSIONS AND BECOME OUR SLAVE, OR WE KILL YOU

HMM... TRICKY ONE

Of course, a lot of people didn't enjoy being slaves. They argued with the Spartans in the only language the Spartans knew – the language of violence. They were probably the toughest of the Greek peoples because they were always having to fight to prove how good they were.

But it wasn't enough to train young men to fight. The training started from the day you were born.

Ten foul facts

1 Children were trained for fitness with running, wrestling, throwing quoits and javelins – and that was just the girls!

2 Girls also had to strip for processions, dances and temple services. That way they wouldn't learn to show off with fine clothes.

3 The marriage custom of Sparta was for a young man to pretend to carry his bride off by violence. The bride then cut off her hair and dressed like a man. The bridegroom rejoined the army and had to sneak off to visit his new wife.

4 A new-born baby was taken to be examined by the oldest Spartans. If it looked fit and strong they said, 'Let it live.' If it looked a bit sickly it was taken up a mountain and left to die.

5 A child didn't belong to its parents – it belonged to the State of Sparta. At the age of seven a child was sent off to join a 'herd' of children. The toughest child was allowed to become leader and order the others about. The old men who watched over them often set the children fighting amongst each other to see who was the toughest.

6 At the age of 12 they were allowed a cloak but no tunic. They were only allowed a bath a few times a year.

7 Children slept on rushes that they gathered from the river bank themselves. If they were cold in winter then they mixed a few thistles in with the reeds ... the prickling gave them a feeling of warmth.

8 The Spartan children were kept hungry. They were then encouraged to steal food – sneakiness is a good skill if you're out on a battlefield. If they were caught stealing they'd be beaten. They weren't beaten for stealing, you understand – they were beaten for being careless enough to get caught. Sometimes the young men were beaten just to toughen them up. If the beating killed the youth then it was just bad luck.

9 Older boys had younger boys to serve them. If the younger boy did something wrong then a common punishment was a bite on the back of the hand.

10 If you cried out while you were fighting then not only were you punished but your best friend was punished as well.

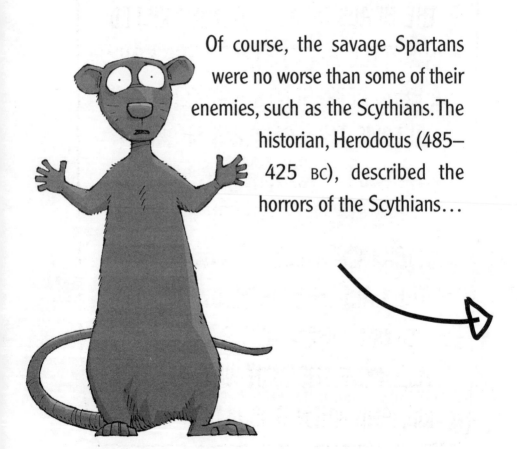

Of course, the savage Spartans were no worse than some of their enemies, such as the Scythians. The historian, Herodotus (485– 425 BC), described the horrors of the Scythians…

IN A WAR, IT IS THE CUSTOM OF A
SCYTHIAN SOLDIER TO DRINK THE
BLOOD OF THE FIRST MAN HE KILLS.
THE HEADS OF ALL ENEMIES KILLED
IN BATTLE ARE TAKEN TO THE KING;
A HEAD REPRESENTS A TOKEN WHICH
ALLOWS THE SOLDIER A SHARE IN
THE LOOT — NO HEAD NO LOOT. HE
STRIPS THE SKIN OFF THE HEAD BY
MAKING A CIRCULAR CUT ROUND
THE EARS AND SHAKING OUT THE
SKULL; THEN HE SCRAPES THE
FLESH OFF THE SKIN WITH AN OX'S
RIB, AND WHEN IT IS CLEAN WORKS

IT SUPPLE WITH HIS FINGERS. HE HANGS THESE TROPHIES ON THE BRIDLE OF HIS HORSE LIKE HANDKERCHIEFS AND IS VERY PROUD OF THEM. THE FINEST WARRIOR IS THE ONE WHO HAS THE MOST SCALPS. MANY SCYTHIANS SEW SCALPS TOGETHER TO MAKE CLOAKS AND WEAR THEM LIKE THE CLOAK OF A PEASANT.

The boy who didn't cry 'fox'

One Spartan story shows you how peculiar the Spartans really were. It's a story about a good little Spartan boy.

How to be a good Spartan 1: Pinch whatever you like – but don't get caught

He stole a fox cub belonging to somebody else.

How to be a good Spartan 2: Don't give up without a struggle

The boy was seen running away from the scene of the theft and arrested. But before they caught him he just had time to stuff the fox cub up his tunic.

How to be a good Spartan 3: Cheat, lie and trick your way out of trouble

The boy's master asked the boy where the fox cub was. The boy replied, 'Fox cub? What fox cub? I don't know anything about a fox cub!'

How to be a good Spartan 4: It's better to be a dead hero than a live whinger

The master's questioning went on ... and on. Until suddenly the boy fell down. Dead. When the guards examined the body they found the fox cub had eaten its way into the boy's guts. The tough Spartan lad hadn't given any sign that he was suffering and he hadn't given in, even though it cost him his life.

Could you be as boldly deceitful as the Spartan boy?

Thermopylae

The story of the boy and the fox might not be true – it simply shows the sort of people the Spartans admired. But the story of the battle of Thermopylae is almost certainly true. Again it shows the Spartans dying rather than giving in.

There were just 300 Spartans led by King Leonidas defending the narrow pass of Thermopylae against tens of thousands of Persians. The Persian leader, Xerxes, sent spies to report how many soldiers were defending the pass. He couldn't believe the Spartans would be daft enough to fight and die. Xerxes didn't know the Spartans.

But the Spartans were not just unafraid. They were really cool about it. They spent the time before the battle oiling their bodies and combing their hair – now that was groovy.

How to be a good Spartan 5: When you're in trouble, think of something witty to say

The Spartans were warned that the Persians had so many archers that their arrows would blot out the sun. Dioneces, the Spartan general, said, 'That's good. We'll have a bit of shade to fight the battle.'

How to be a good Spartan 6: Stay cooler than an ice lolly

The Spartans held on for a week. Then a traitor guided the Persians to a secret pathway that led them behind the Spartans. The 300 Spartans were massacred. As they fought to the death some lost their swords. They battled on with their fists and their teeth.

Could you stay as cool as a Spartan in danger?

YOU'RE LATE!

WELL, THERE'S EIGHT OF US IN THE FAMILY AND THE ALARM WAS SET FOR SEVEN...

"DID YOU KNOW...?
ONE HORRIBLE HISTORICAL WAY OF PROVING YOU WERE A GOOD SPARTAN WAS TO BE WHIPPED AT THE ALTAR OF THE GOD, ARTEMIS. THE ONE WHO SUFFERED THE MOST LASHES WAS THE TOUGHEST. BLEEDING HALF TO

DEATH – SOMETIMES ALL THE WAY TO DEATH – BUT TOUGH. AH YES, A PERFECT SPARTAN. *"*

The spooky Spartan

Pausanius was a great Spartan general who helped to defeat the Persians in 479 BC. But the Spartans thought he was getting too big-headed and they asked him to return to Sparta to explain – or be punished.

Pausanius was not amused. He wrote to the Persian king, Xerxes, and offered to betray Sparta. Off went the messenger to Xerxes. But that messenger wondered why other messengers before him hadn't come back. So he opened the letter and read it. There on the end was a little message for Xerxes...

The messenger took the letter to the Spartans instead of to Xerxes – wouldn't you? The Spartans sent a force to kill Pausanius. The general fled to the temple of Athena where he sheltered in a small building. 'You can't lay a finger on me here. I'm on sacred ground,' he said.

'Right,' the leader of the assassins said. 'We won't lay a finger on you.' And they didn't. They just bricked up the door and left him to starve to death. That should have been the end of Pausanius. The trouble was his ghost started wandering round the temple making such hideous noises that the priestess was losing customers. In the end she sent for a magician — a sort of groovy Greek Ghostbuster — to get rid of him … finally.

The Odd Athenians

Deadly Draco

The people of Athens were very different from the Spartans. One of their first rulers was a man called Draco. The Athenians thought the Spartans were pretty brutal, but the laws of Draco were nearly as cruel. He wrote the first law book for Athens, and criminals were executed for almost any crime. Under Draco's laws…

• you could have someone made your personal slave if they owed you money

• the theft of an apple or a cabbage was punishable by death

• people found guilty of idleness would be executed.

Draco said…

YES IT'S UNFAIR. LITTLE CRIMES AND BIG CRIMES GET THE SAME PUNISHMENT. IF ONLY I COULD THINK OF A PUNISHMENT WORSE THAN DEATH FOR THE SERIOUS ONES.

Seven hundred years later a Greek writer, Plutarch, said…

DRACO'S LAWS WERE NOT WRITTEN IN INK BUT IN BLOOD.

Other Greeks thought that Draco's laws were better than no laws. (The people who thought this were not the ones who Draco had executed, of course.)

Playful Peisistratus

Another ruler, Peisistratus, wasn't so quite so harsh. He was still a 'tyrant' – in Greece that was someone who took control of the state by force – but he stayed there only as long as the people agreed with what he was doing.

Peisistratus made the people pay heavy taxes – ten per cent of all they earned – but at least he had a sense of humour.

One day he visited a farmer. The farmer didn't recognize Peisistratus.

Peisistratus laughed – and ordered that the old farmer need never pay taxes again.

Plotting Peisistratus

Peisistratus became very unpopular and the people of Athens were turning against him. Then one day he drove his cart into the market place in a terrible state. He and his mules were cut and bleeding.

'I've been attacked by assassins!' he cried. 'I barely escaped with my life.'

The Athenians were worried they would lose their leader – not a popular leader, but the only leader they had. They organized the strongest and most brutal Athenian men to be his bodyguards. He then used them to seize control of the city.

The attack on Peisistratus had put him in power. Just as he meant it to. For there had been *no* attack. The crafty leader had simply made the wounds himself!

Who killed the ox?

The Athenians weren't as ruthless as the Spartans. But they had their own funny little ways. One of the strangest customs of Athens involved the sacrifice of an ox in the temple. Killing the ox wasn't strange in itself. It's what the Athenians did *afterwards* that was curious. They held a trial to decide, 'Who killed the ox?'

Horrible hemlock

The Athenians didn't just have strange ways of killing knives. They also killed each other in unusual ways.

After they had lost the war with Sparta, the Athenians looked for someone to blame. They blamed the old teacher, Socrates. Being a rather groovy guy, he was always hanging around with young people, telling them not to believe in the old gods. (That's a bit like your own teacher telling you not to believe in Father Christmas.) In Athens this was punishable by death.

But the Athenians didn't kill the old teacher – they told him to kill himself with poison! Plato described the gruesome scene ...

The man who was to give the poison came in with it ready mixed in a cup. Socrates saw him and said, 'Good Sir, you understand these things. What do I have to do?'

'Just drink it and walk around until your legs begin to feel heavy, then lie down. It works very quickly.'

The man gave Socrates the cup.

The teacher took it cheerfully, without trembling, and without even turning pale. He just looked at the man and said, 'May I drink a toast?'

'You may,' the man replied.

'Then I drink to the gods and pray that we will be just as happy after death as we were in life.'

Then he drank the poison quickly and cheerfully. Until then most of us had held back our tears. But when we saw him drinking, the tears came in floods.

I covered my face and wept – not for him but for myself; I had lost such a good friend.

Socrates looked at us and said sternly, 'I have heard that a person should be allowed to die in silence. So control yourselves and be quiet.' We stopped crying.

The teacher lay down. The man with the poison squeezed his foot. Socrates said he felt nothing. He said that when the poison reached the heart he would be gone.

As the numbness reached his waist Socrates called to young Crito. He said, 'Crito, we owe Asclepius a sacrifice. Be sure you pay him. Don't forget.'

[Asclepius was the god of healing.]

'Of course,' Crito replied. 'Is there anything else you want?'

But Socrates didn't reply.

This was the end of our friend.

The best, wisest and most honest person I have ever known.

What a hero! Probably the only teacher in history to die so nobly. Would your teacher be as brave?

Unfortunately you'll never have the chance to find out …Boots the Chemist does not sell hemlock.

Dreadful democracy

Most countries today are run as *democracies* – that is to say every adult has a vote on which laws are passed and how the government spends its money. Athens, being really groovy, had the first democracy. But because they still had a lot to learn, they didn't quite get it right…

The Power of the Persians

King Darius of Persia had a large army and decided it was about time he took over Greece as well. He didn't bother going to the battle personally – he thought the Greeks would be a pushover. They *should* have been a pushover because …

• there was only the Athenian army to stop them – the Spartans were too busy at a religious festival and they missed the battle.

• the Greek soldiers were a bit frightened by the appearance of the Persian soldiers.

The Persians were wearing *trousers* while the Greeks wore groovy *skirts*.

Still, the Athenian Greeks won the great battle at a place called Marathon.

That kept the Persians away for about ten years.

Then along came the new Persian king, Xerxes, with an absolutely *huge* army.

There were too many soldiers to transport across the Hellespont – a stretch of water almost 1,200 metres wide between Greece and Persia – so Xerxes built a bridge.

A storm came and smashed the bridge. Xerxes was cross – yes, I know there are *two* crosses in Xerxes, but I don't mean that sort of cross. He was furious.

#!!*✡!

MORE LIKE *BERSERXES* IF YOU ASK ME

So, what did the potty Persian do?

1 Ordered the bridge builder to be given three hundred lashes.

2 Ordered the sea at Hellespont to receive three hundred lashes.

3 Ordered the army to swim across.

Answer

2 Xerxes ordered that the sea should receive lashes and have iron shackles thrown in as punishment. One story even said he sent torturers to brand the sea with burning irons.

Paper-headed Persians

The Greeks wouldn't have feared the Persians so much if they'd known what the great historian Herodotus knew. He told a remarkable story about an earlier Persian battlefield – at Pelusium in Egypt where the Persians had fought in 525 BC.

ON THE BATTLEFIELD I SAW A STRANGE THING WHICH THE NATIVES POINTED OUT TO ME. THE BONES OF THE DEAD LAY SCATTERED ON THE FIELD IN TWO LOTS – THOSE OF THE PERSIANS AND THOSE OF THE EGYPTIANS. IF THEN, YOU STRIKE A PERSIAN SKULL (EVEN WITH A PEBBLE) THEY ARE SO WEAK YOU WILL BREAK A HOLE IN THEM. BUT THE EGYPTIAN SKULLS ARE SO STRONG THAT YOU MAY HIT THEM WITH A ROCK AND HARDLY CRACK THEM.

The wooden wall

After slaughtering the Spartans, Xerxes headed south towards Athens. The Athenians retreated to the island of Salamis, just off the coast of Athens. They had to watch while Xerxes burned Athens to the ground.

But the Athenian leader was a groovy Greek called Themistocles. He went to the temple at Delphi and asked for advice from the 'Oracle' – a kind of adviser on behalf of the gods. The Oracle told him to 'put his trust in the wooden wall'. What did he do?

1 Built a navy (of wooden ships).

2 Built a wooden fence around the island of Salamis to keep the Persians out.

3 Built a wooden fence around Athens to keep the Persians in.

Answer

1 Themistocles guessed that he should put his faith in his navy – and he got it right. The 800 Persian ships were attacked in the narrow waters between Salamis and Athens by just 310 Greek ships. The Greeks had bronze rams on their bows that smashed and sank the Persians.

The spooky ship of Salamis

Herodotus also reported a strange happening at the battle of Salamis...

The Athenians tell this story about a captain from Corinth called Adeimantus. As the battle started he was filled with fear and dread; he hoisted his sails and hurried from the fight. When the other Corinthians saw this they turned to follow him. But just as they reached the temple of Athena on Salamis, a ship came alongside them. It was a ship of the gods for no man sent it. A voice from the strange ship called, 'Would you betray your Greek friends, Adeimantus? They are now winning the battle. Turn back and help.' The Corinthian said it was a lie. The voice replied, 'You can take this ship and destroy it if you find out I am lying. Turn back, turn back.' So Adeimantus and the Corinthians joined the battle again and helped the Greeks to win. But no one was able to tell him where the strange ship had come from...

Maybe it was a 'ghost ship'. Another story says the Corinthians only *pretended* to run away. It was all part of a cunning Athenian plan. The Corinthians' trick led the Persians into a trap. They then turned and attacked them when they least expected it. There never was a ship of the gods.

Which story do you believe? One fact is that lots of sailors died. Two horrible historical epitaphs read...

> HE WENT DOWN WITH HIS SHIP AND WHERE HIS BONES ARE ROTTING ONLY THE SEABIRD KNOWS

And...

SAILORS, DON'T ASK WHOSE BODY LIES HERE. I WISH YOU BETTER LUCK THAN MINE AND A KINDER SEA

Peloponnesian wars

Xerxes the Persian went home after he lost the sea battle at Salamis. His son-in-law, Mardonius, wanted to stay and batter a few more Greeks, so Xerxes left him to get on with it. Mardonius was killed and his army defeated.

Of course, the Athenians were really pleased with themselves. They decided to get all the Greek states to team up in case the Persians ever came back. The trouble was the Athenians wanted to be the captain of the team.

Sparta weren't having that. They decided not to play. After that it was just a matter of time before Athens and Sparta fought each other to see who was best. And that was the start of the Peloponnesian War.

Awful armies

Alcibiades was a great Athenian general – but a terrible poser. He dressed in the grooviest clothes and would do anything to draw attention to himself. Once he cut off the tail of his favourite dog so that people would take notice.

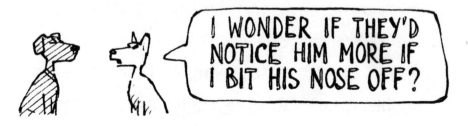

I WONDER IF THEY'D NOTICE HIM MORE IF I BIT HIS NOSE OFF?

Half of Athens (especially the women) loved him but the men in power hated him and wanted him dead. They sent him off to fight the Spartans while they plotted against him.

Alcibiades led the Athenian army in the attack on the Spartan allies at Syracuse (in Sicily) between 415 and 413 BC. But he was called back to Athens because he was charged with 'sacrilege' – that's being nasty to the gods. He was supposed to have gone to some statues of gods and knocked off their noses – and (because the statues didn't have any clothes on) he knocked off their 'naughty bits' as well.

Of course, clever Alcibiades knew they'd probably kill him for this. So he didn't go back to Athens, sensible man. He went over to the enemy – Sparta. He told the Spartans all the secrets of the Athenian army. The Spartans went and helped Syracuse.

THE PELOPONNESIAN WAR LEAGUE RESULTS

SPARTA & SYRACUSE UNITED [1] - ATHENS [0]

Of course, Alcibiades came to a sticky end – just like the tail of his dog, really! The Spartans had him assassinated rather than let him switch back to fighting for Athens.

A group of men arrived at his house to kill him but hadn't the nerve to fight him face to face – even though they outnumbered him. First they set his house on fire. When Alcibiades came out into the open, carrying his sword, they shot him full of arrows from a safe distance.

Wonderful weapons

During the Peloponnesian wars, Greeks were fighting Greeks. If you know how your enemy fights, you can stop him – and at the same time he can stop you. Every battle becomes a 0-0 draw. What you need are some secret weapons to surprise and frighten the enemy.

That's what the groovy Greek army from Boetia came up with. Here's what they made…

TOP SECRET

THE BOETIAN BLASTER

1 CUT DOWN A TALL STRAIGHT TREE, TRIM THE BRANCHES OFF THEN SPLIT THE TRUNK IN TWO

2 HOLLOW OUT THE TRUNK THEN JOIN THE TWO HALVES TOGETHER, YOU NOW HAVE A HOLLOW TUBE LIKE A FLUTE

3 HANG A METAL VESSEL FULL OF SMOULDERING COALS, TAR AND SULPHUR AT ONE END AND A BELLOWS AT THE OTHER END

4 CARRY THE MACHINE TO A PLACE WHERE THE ENEMY WALLS ARE MOSTLY MADE OF WOOD. AIM THE TUBE AT THE WALLS AND SQUEEZE THE BELLOWS.

PROTECTION FROM ENEMY ARROWS

5 A HUGE FLAME WILL SHOOT OUT OF THE METAL VESSEL, SETTING FIRE TO THE WALLS AND DRIVING THE DEFENDERS AWAY

It worked! The Boetians captured the city of Delium with it. They had invented the world's first *flame thrower!*

Alexander the Great-er

Just when the Persian threat to Greece had begun to fade, a new one came from a small kingdom in the north of Greece called Macedon. Some historians have even said that Macedon wasn't Greek at all.

First came Philip, king of Macedon. He defeated the Athenians and then told them he wanted them to attack the old enemy ... Persia.

Then there was a small hitch in Philip's plan ... he died. But that was only a tiny complication for the plan. (A rather bigger complication for Philip, of course.) Philip's son was greater and even groovier than him. Alexander the Great-er in fact...

Alexander – This is Your Life

YOU WERE BORN, ALEXANDER, IN 356 BC: THE GREATEST GREEK EVER

DON'T CALL ME A *GREEK*, SUNSHINE. THE THE GREEKS CALLED MY DAD A BARBARIAN

YET YOU ADMIRED THE GREEK HEROES. YOU LOVED HOMER'S POETRY SO MUCH YOU CARRIED HIS STORY OF TROY EVERYWHERE. YOUR OLD TEACHER ARISTOTLE TOLD US

HE SLEPT WITH IT UNDER HIS PILLOW ACTUALLY

AND YOU HAD YOUR CHANCE WHEN YOU WERE JUST TWENTY YEARS OLD. YOUR FATHER, KING PHILIP DIED. TONIGHT WE PROUDLY PRESENT HIS GHOST...

DIED. I WAS MURDERED. STABBED BY MY OWN BODYGUARD. AND I THINK I KNOW WHO PUT HIM UP TO IT, ALEXANDER. IT WAS Y...

I DENY IT!

The knotty problem

Alexander entered Gordium and was told that the wagon of King Gordius was tied to its shafts with a knot that no one could untie. A legend said that the man who finally untied it would rule all Asia. How did Alexander unfasten the wagon from its shafts?

Answer

He took out his sword and cut through the knot.

Think Like a Greek

The Greeks were very superstitious people. They believed in horoscopes and ghosts and the gods deciding your fate. They believed that the gods spoke through 'Oracles' and you could learn about the future ... if you understood the Oracle.

Awesome Oracles

The Greeks liked to know what would happen in the future. They didn't have crystal balls or people reading your palm. Instead they had Oracles. You went to a holy place, made a sacrifice and asked a god to tell you what the future held.

Of course, the god didn't speak to a human directly. There were a couple of ways of getting your message. At Delphi, the god Apollo spoke through his Oracle priestess. She was a bit like a medium in a seance today. She went into a trance and spoke in a strange language. The priests then took this baffling information and told the visitor what it meant.

The priests at Delphi actually could give good advice. So many visitors came, with so much gossip, that the priests of Delphi knew more than most people about what was going on in the Greek states.

Croesus the crafty

There were several Oracles in Greece. Crafty King Croesus decided to test them to see which was the most accurate.

He sent seven messengers to seven Oracles. They all had to ask the same question at the same time ... *What is King Croesus doing at this very moment?* They brought their replies back to the king. The Oracle of Delphi's answer was a curious one. It said...

MY SENSES SMELL THE STRANGEST SMELL
A TORTOISE COOKING IN ITS SHELL
A LAMB THAT'S COOKING, BUBBLING HOT
WITHIN A COVERED BRASSY POT

Croesus was impressed. He'd deliberately chosen the daftest thing he could think of to do on that day. So he cut up a tortoise and a lamb and made a stew of them. He cooked them in a brass cauldron with a lid.

Croesus decided the Oracle of Delphi was the one to believe. Crafty Croesus. But…

Double-crossed Croesus

But the priests also cheated a bit. They gave curious answers that could mean more than one thing. King Croesus of Lydia spoke to the Oracle when he was about to go to war with Persia.

'What will happen if I attack Persia?' King Croesus asked.

'In the battle a great empire will be destroyed,' the Oracle said.

Croesus went off happily into battle – and lost! Lydia was destroyed. He thought the Oracle meant that *Persia* would be destroyed.

Some of the Greeks' favourite stories were about the Oracle. Many were about the ancient game of…

Beat the Oracle

The Bacchiad family ruled Corinth. They were rich and powerful … and they were worried. Big Bacchiad had just come back from the Oracle with a threatening message.

'The Oracle has said, "Labda will give birth to a rock that will roll down on those who rule and he will put all Corinth right,"' Big Bacchiad told them.

'Put all Corinth right?' Mrs Bacchiad sniffed.

'Nothing wrong with Corinth … at least, not while we're in charge.'

'That's not the point,' Little Bacchiad pointed out. 'If the gods say it's curtains for us, then it's curtains for us.'

'Hah! Just like a man, talking like that. Listen, if the Oracle says she's giving birth to the child who'll defeat us, we simply kill the child.'

'That's murder that is,' Big Bacchiad frowned. 'We'd never get away with it.'

'Not if the baby has an *accident*,' Mrs Bacchiad grinned an evil grin.

'Not much chance of that,' Little Bacchiad sighed.

'Oh, but there is if we *make* it have an accident,' the woman explained. 'As soon as the baby is born, we go visiting. Ask to see the new baby.'

'That's nice,' Big Bacchiad said.

'No it's not,' Mrs Bacchiad said with a slow shake

of the head. 'Whoever she hands the baby to will drop it.'

'Drop it!' Little Bacchiad squeaked.

'On the stone floor,' the woman said grimly. 'On its head. End of problem.'

Of course it wasn't that simple. With the Oracle it never is. The baby was born and the Bacchiads went to visit. Mrs Bacchiad left the house ten minutes later. Her face was white with bright red spots of anger on her chubby cheeks.

'I cannot believe it. All you had to do was drop the baby. *Drop the baby!* That's what we agreed. Why did you not drop it?'

Big Bacchaid gave a faint and sheepish smile. 'It smiled at me. I couldn't drop the little feller while he was smiling at me, could I? I hadn't the heart.'

'Heart? It's not heart you're short of – it's brain,' the woman seethed. She turned to Little Bacchiad. 'Tonight you go back with a club. You creep into the house and you kill the child. Understand?'

Little Bacchiad nodded. 'I won't let you down,' he promised.

But Labda had seen Mrs Bacchiad's face when the man handed the baby back to her. She knew the woman wanted the baby dead. So that night she hid the child in a wooden chest. It slept safely and woke the next day still smiling.

Labda called the baby Cypselus – after the word meaning chest. Cypselus grew up a popular and groovy leader, while the Bacchiad family were hated in Corinth. The young man became king of Corinth – a strong king but a good-natured one. However, when it came to the Bacchiads he was quite, quite ruthless.

Cypselus was the rock that would roll down on those who ruled ... and, like a rock, he crushed them. Just as the Oracle predicted.

"DID YOU KNOW... ?
THE PYTHIAN ORACLE AT DELPHI
INHALED SMOKE FROM THE BURNING
LEAVES OF CERTAIN TREES TO HELP
THEM SEE INTO THE FUTURE. THE
LEAVES GAVE OFF A
DRUG THAT PUT
THEM INTO A
TRANCE.
BUT AT THE CORINTH
ORACLE THERE WERE
CHEATS AT WORK. THERE
YOU COULD ACTUALLY

SPEAK DIRECTLY TO A GOD! YOU SPOKE TO THE ALTAR ... AND A VOICE BOOMED BACK FROM BENEATH YOUR FEET WITH THE ANSWER. WAS IT A MIRACLE? THE VISITORS BELIEVED IT WAS. BUT TODAY'S ARCHAEOLOGISTS KNOW BETTER. THEY FOUND A SECRET TUNNEL THAT LED UNDER THE ALTAR. A PRIEST COULD CRAWL ALONG AND LIE UNDER THE FEET OF THE VISITOR. HE COULD LISTEN TO THE QUESTIONS AND SPEAK AN ANSWER THROUGH A FUNNEL INTO A TUBE. "

Greek superstitions

The Greeks had some of the cleverest thinkers of ancient times. Yet, in some ways, they had some very strange beliefs.

People today are nervous about walking under a ladder because they think it will bring them bad luck, or they touch wood to bring them good luck. The Greeks had their own strange superstitions. They believed…

1 Birds were messengers between earth and heaven, and the moon was a resting place for spirits on their way to heaven.

2 The Greeks believed that Hecate was the goddess of witchcraft and crossroads. She would appear at crossroads on clear nights, along with ghosts and howling phantom dogs. The Greeks left food at crossroads for her. (She was also asked for help with curing madness – the Greeks believed madness was caused by the spirits of the dead.)

3 The Greeks looked at the guts of dead birds and believed they could read the future from them.

4 They also thought there were spirits called 'daimons' around. Some were good and protected you; some were evil and could lead you into wickedness. Even clever people like Socrates believed in daimons. His own daimon warned him of trouble ahead ... and it never let him down.

WHAT DO THEY SAY?

IN THE FUTURE THERE WILL BE FEWER BIRDS

IT WASN'T ME SIR, IT WAS MY DAIMON

5 Sometimes the Greeks kept dead bodies in jars called *pithos*. But sometimes, they said, the spirits of the dead escaped from the jars and began to bother the living with illness and disease. These wicked spirits were called *keres*. The best way to stop the keres from getting into your house was to paint tar round your door frames. That way the keres would stick to the tar and not be able to get into the house.

6 The Greeks believed that if you dreamed about seeing your reflection in a mirror then you would die soon after. But don't worry, because you would soon be born again. According to some Greeks you are in three parts…

• body • soul • mind

③ THE SOUL POPS OFF TO THE MOON AND THE MIND TO THE SUN

② THE SOUL AND MIND THEN GO TO THE UNDERWORLD WHERE THERE IS A SECOND DEATH AND THEY ARE SEPARATED

④ THEY ARE BOTH RE-BORN AND JOIN UP AGAIN ON THE MOON

① WHEN YOU DIE THEN THE BODY IS SEPARATED FROM THE OTHER TWO BITS AND GOES BACK TO DUST

⑤ THEY THEN GO BACK TO EARTH AND PICK UP A NEW BODY

7 They also believed that the left side is bad – the right side is good. Many people still believe that today – they try to force left-handed children to write with their right hand, for example.

Potty Pythagoras

The famous teacher, Pythagoras, set up his own religion. The Pythagoreans believed that the soul lived on after death and went into another body. One day Pythagoras saw a man beating a dog and heard it yelping. He told the man…

'STOP! STOP! THAT'S MY DEAR FRIEND. I RECOGNISE HIS VOICE!'

In fact it wasn't safe to have anything to do with butchers or huntsmen – when they killed that cow or that deer they may have murdered your dead mother.

They also thought that if they behaved themselves they might come back as a great person. If they were naughty in this life they'd come back as something nasty – a pig, a dog, even a tree. And if you were really, really wicked you'd come back as the worst thing of all … a woman!

The Pythagoreans lived apart from the rest of the Greek people and had some rather strange rules. Does your teacher have strange rules? Then ask them which of these rules Pythagoras truly had ... and which are false.

True or False

1 Don't eat beans.

2 Don't walk along the main street.

3 Don't touch the fire with an iron poker.

4 Don't touch a white cockerel.

5 Don't eat the heart of an animal.

6 Don't stand on your fingernail clippings.

7 Don't leave the mark of your body on a bed when you get up.

8 Don't look in a mirror beside a lamp.

9 Help a man to load something – but don't help anyone to unload.

10 Don't pick your nose with the fingers of your left hand.

Answers

10 is false. All the rest are true. Some Greeks believed that beans contained the souls of the dead and would never eat them.

Think like a Greek

In the summer of 413 BC the army of Athens was in trouble. They were trying to beat the town of Syracuse with a siege. But one of their leaders had been killed and the other leader, Nicias, was poorly with a fever.

The Athenians decided to pack up and go home. Everyone agreed this was a good idea and they began packing to go. But that night there was an eclipse of the full moon. The soldiers said this was a sign from the gods.

A sign of disaster, some said. A sign that they should stay … or a sign that they should go? They couldn't agree. They asked their leader, Nicias.

'We will forget any plan to return home. We must wait for the next full moon,' Nicias said.

He waited 27 more days. What happened?

1 Nicias died and the army went home.

2 They suffered disaster anyway.

3 The Syracuse army surrendered.

Answer

2 The extra 27 days gave the Syracuse navy time to block off the river with rows of ships chained together. The Athenian ships couldn't get out of the river to get their army back home. Their army had to march across the land instead. The enemy were waiting and the Athenian army was wiped out. The ones who weren't killed were made into slaves. This disaster was the end of Athens as a great state ... and all because of an eclipse of the moon and the superstitious nature of a Greek general.

Live Like a Greek

Polybius' Checkerboard

The Greeks were also very groovy with numbers. Polybius, born in 200 BC, was a Greek historian of Rome. He was one of 1,000 hostages taken to Rome in 168 BC. His main history books contained 40 volumes, but he also had time to invent this code, now known as Polybius' Checkerboard.

Each letter has a pair of numbers – the horizontal (across) number followed by the vertical (up-down). So, 'B' is 1-2, but F is 2-1. The word 'Yes' is 54 15 43. Get it?

	1	2	3	4	5
1	A	B	C	D	E
2	F	G	H	I/J	K
3	L	M	N	O	P
4	Q	R	S	T	U
5	V	W	X	Y	Z

Then work out this…

44 23 15 22 42 15 15 25 44 I5 11 13 23 15 42
11 33 11 53 24 32 11 33 14 15 42 12 42 34 45
22 23 44 44 23 15 21 24 42 43 44 43 45 33 –
14 24 11 31 44 34 22 42 I5 I5 13 I5.

3I, 0I, 44, 15, 1I, 22, 1I, 24, 33, 12, 34, 54

The Greek teacher Anaximander brought the
first sun-dial to Greece.

"DID YOU KNOW...?
POLYBIUS' CHECKERBOARD MAY
HAVE BEEN A GOOD WAY OF
SENDING SECRET MESSAGES. BUT
A GREEK CALLED HISTIAEUS
FOUND A BETTER ONE!
HE WAS IMPRISONED BY
THE PERSIANS BUT WAS
ALLOWED TO SEND A LETTER TO
HIS COUSIN ARISTAGORAS. THE
PERSIANS STUDIED THE
MESSAGE CAREFULLY. THEY
COULD SEE NO CODE OR

SECRET MEANING. THE MESSAGE WAS
A PERFECTLY HARMLESS LETTER.
THEY LET A SLAVE TAKE THE LETTER
TO ARISTAGORAS.
AS SOON AS THE SLAVE ARRIVED
HE SAID TO ARISTAGORAS, 'SHAVE
MY HEAD.' ARISTAGORAS SHAVED
THE SLAVE'S HEAD. TATTOOED ON
HIS SCALP WAS THE REAL MESSAGE.
'LEAD A REBELLION AGAINST THE
PERSIANS.' COOL, EH?"

SCRAPE
SCRAPE

WE MUST
BE A
WHOLE
BOOK!

Make a pinhole camera

The Greeks also invented other groovy devices which are still important to us today. One of the cleverest was the camera obscura – or the 'pinhole' camera. A Greek artist covered a window with a dark material, then punched a small hole through. An upside-down image of the scene was seen on the inside wall and traced by the artist.

You could have a go at making your own, slightly smaller version:

1 Make a box of black card, **20** x **10** x **10** cm.

2 Make a small pinhole in black paper at one end.

3 Place grease-proof paper across the other end.

4 Hold it up to a bright scene.

The scene will be 'projected' on to the grease-proof paper.

Note: this image will be upside down – you may have to stand on your head to get the best view!

Let the punishment fit the crime

Alexandria was a city in Egypt but ruled by the Greeks. Around 250 BC they had a set of laws which might give some idea of how the Greek law worked. Can you match the crime to the punishment? Just remember the law wasn't completely fair. Especially if you were a slave.

Crime

1 A free man strikes another free man or free woman.

2 A slave strikes a free man or free woman.

3 A drunk person injures somebody else.

4 A free man threatens another with wood, iron or bronze.

5 A slave threatens another with wood, iron or bronze.

Punishment

a) A hundred lashes

b) Fine of 100 drachmas

c) A hundred lashes

d) Fine of 100 drachmas

e) Fine of 200 drachmas

1d) 2c) 3e) 4b) 5a)

If a master didn't want his slave to receive the 100 lashes then he had to pay 200 drachma, or 2 drachma a blow.

If you argued with a fine then you could go to court. But be careful. If you lost then you had to pay double for crime 1 or treble for crime 4.

Woe for women

Being a slave in ancient Greece wasn't much fun. Being a woman wasn't too groovy either. The Spartan women lived like men – the Athenian women lived like slaves. They were told what to do and what not to do – and they didn't have anything like the freedom that the free men enjoyed...

GREEK GOOD WIFE GUIDE

A WOMAN SHOULD	A WOMAN DOES NOT
• STAY AT HOME • BE BROUGHT UP WITH SLAVES AND LEARN HOUSEHOLD SKILLS • LEARN TO SPIN, WEAVE, COOK AND MANAGE SLAVES • HAVE A HUSBAND – CHOSEN BY HER FATHER – WHEN SHE IS 15 • WORSHIP THE GODDESS HESTIA	• VOTE • BUY OR SELL ANYTHING WORTH MORE THAN A SMALL MEASURE OF BARLEY • OWN ANYTHING OTHER THAN HER CLOTHES, JEWELLERY AND SLAVES • LEAVE THE HOUSE EXCEPT TO VISIT OTHER WOMEN OR GO TO RELIGIOUS FESTIVALS AND FUNERALS

Groovy girls

The women of Attica, the region surrounding Athens, were different from the women living in Athens. They helped their husbands in the fields. They also had a curious way of preparing their daughters for marriage.

Girls aged about 13 were sent to the Brauron temple of the goddess, Artemis. There they prepared to be mature young women, and good wives, by doing what?

1 Learning how to fire bows and arrows, to throw spears, to mend armour and sharpen swords.

2 Praying to the goddess for wisdom, and learning the secret spells to keep husbands happy and healthy.

3 Running and dancing through the woods with no clothes on pretending to be she-bears.

3 The idea was they got their wildness 'out of their systems' before they settled down to marriage. The Brauron temple proved very popular with Greek girls around 370–380 BC.

However, girls, you should *not* try this at your local place of worship – you'd only get arrested, or photographed by the boys in your class, or catch pneumonia … or all three.

I'M BEGINNING TO REALLY ENJOY GREEK HISTORY

TEST YOUR TEACHER

Teachers don't know everything — they just try to kid you that they do. Test their true brain power with these questions on the groovy Greeks…

1 Aristotle the great Greek teacher had a favourite meat. What was it?
a) camel
b) turkey
c) horse liver

2 The great playwright, Aeschylus, is supposed to have died when an eagle flew over

his head and dropped something
on it. What did the eagle drop?
a) a tortoise
b) a hare
c) a stone

3 As well as the Olympic games
there were games in Isthmia.
The winners at the Isthmian

games were given a crown as a prize. What was the crown made of?
a) celery
b) rhubarb
c) gold

4 Before clever Aristotle came along, the Greeks had a strange belief about elephants. What was it?
a) an elephant has no knee joints so it goes to sleep leaning against a tree
b) elephants never forget
c) eating elephant meat makes you strong

5 Which team sport did the Ancient Greeks enjoy that we still play today?
a) hockey
b) soccer
c) volleyball

6 The Greek teacher, gorgeous Gorgias, said that 'nothing exists' … not even himself. He nearly didn't. He had a peculiar birth. Where was he born?

a) in his dead mother's coffin
b) on a mountain in a snow storm
c) on board a sinking ship

7 The Spartan youths tried out their military training by doing what for their town?
a) becoming secret police and murdering troublemakers
b) mending roads and keeping the streets clean
c) becoming servants in old people's homes and cooking for them

8 How far did the Greek explorer, Pytheas, sail?
a) Britain and the North Sea
b) Crete in the Mediterranean
c) America and the Atlantic

9 The Greeks invented a new weapon in the 4th century BC. They set fire to inflammable liquids then threw them over enemy ships or enemy cities. What is this weapon called?

a) Greek fire

b) Zeus's revenge

c) flaming dangerous

10 A sacred plant was sprinkled on graves. But we don't consider it sacred today. What is it?

a) parsley

b) cabbage

c) garlic

Answers

The answer to every question is **a)**.

- If your teacher scored 0 to 5 they need to go back to school.
- 6 to 9 is pretty good.
- If they scored 10 they probably cheated and read the book before you did.

Test yourself

Now test yourself. See how many answers you can remember by arranging the following into the right order...

A	**B**	**C**
The playwright, Aeschylus,	invented a new weapon called	hockey
A sacred plant	sailed to	a camel
Aristotle, the great Greek teacher	died when hit on the head by	an elephant going to sleep leaning against a tree
A Greek sportsman	was born in	a tortoise
A Greek sailor	was sprinkled on graves and called	the secret police
A Spartan youth	enjoyed the team sport called	celery
The Greek explorer, Pytheas	won a crown made from	Greek fire
The Greek teacher, Gorgias	believed in	the North Sea
A winner at the Isthmian games	trained in	parsley
An early Greek person	enjoyed meat from	his dead mother's coffin

Die Like a Greek

What's up, Doc?

The earliest Greek doctor was said to be called Aesculapius. But, since he was supposed to be the son of a god, he probably didn't exist.

But his followers, the Asculapians, did exist. They didn't work from a hospital, they worked from a temple. Most of their patients recovered with rest, sleep and good food. But Asculapians liked people to think they were gods so the patients had to say prayers and make sacrifices.

The temple was famous because no one ever died in the temple of Aesculapius and his doctor-priests! How did they manage this?

They *cheated.* If someone was dying when they arrived then they weren't allowed in. And if they started dying once they got inside they were dumped in the nearby woods.

The doctor-priests were in it for the money. They warned patients that if they didn't pay, the gods would make them sick again. And they advertised. Carvings in the ruins show the doctor-priests made fantastic claims…

In time, the temples changed into proper medical schools. Later, the great Hippocrates (460–377 BC) came along and said that magical cures by the gods were nonsense. He believed in the proper study of the body, and experiments.

Hippocrates was so great that today's doctors still take the Oath of Hippocrates (though it has been modified during the 20th century) and promise, 'I will give no deadly medicine to anyone if asked ... I will use treatment to help the sick but never to injure.'

Could you take the groovy Greek version of the oath? You would have to swear...

But Hippocrates wasn't perfect. He said there were 91 bones in the body – now we know there are 206!

He also believed in 'bleeding' as a cure. A young man with a rumbling tummy was 'bled' by

Hippocrates until he hardly had any blood left in his body ... and he recovered!

One test for a lung disease was to shake the patient and listen for the splashing inside.

Old Doc Hippo was a bit of a whinger. He complained that, 'If a patient gets worse or dies, people always blame the doctor.'

Still, *you* would complain if you had to do what Hippo had to do. Hippo took samples of...

- **VOMIT**
- **EAR WAX**
- **TEARS**
- **SNOT**
- **PEE**
- **INFECTED WOUNDS**

…and he tested them. But he didn't test them in a laboratory with chemicals the way modern doctors can. He tested them by what?

1 colour

2 boiling them with rhubarb juice

3 tasting them

3 Either the doctor or the patient had to taste the sample.

Hippo and his followers also practised cutting into the skull to drain fluids off the brain. But he wasn't the first to do this ... there is evidence that Stone Age people did this operation. (Would you like to be operated on by a surgeon with a flint axe?)

The superstitious Greeks kept the piece of bone as a good-luck charm. It was supposed to keep you safe from disease.

But Hippo said some things which doctors today, every day, still say to their patients...

FAT PEOPLE DIE SOONER THAN THIN PEOPLE.

Hippo also said how doctors should look and behave…

A DOCTOR MUST BE CAREFUL NOT TO GET TOO FAT. SOMEONE WHO CAN'T LOOK AFTER HIS OWN FITNESS SHOULDN'T BE ALLOWED TO LOOK AFTER OTHER PEOPLE'S.

SECONDLY HE SHOULD BE CLEAN, WEAR GOOD CLOTHES AND USE A SWEET (BUT NOT TOO STRONG) SCENT. THIS IS PLEASANT WHEN VISITING THE SICK.

HE MUST NOT LOOK TOO GRIM OR TOO CHEERFUL — A GRIM MAN WILL WORRY THE PATIENT WHILE A LAUGHING MAN MAY BE SEEN AS AN IDIOT.

And he must have been a good doctor because he lived to the age of 99 years.

Medical monster

Not every doctor was as good and unselfish as Hippocrates. Menecrates of Syracuse was much more grasping and cruel. He was especially fond of really sick patients because he could blackmail them.

Medical manure

Of course, if you didn't want to go to a doctor like Menecrates then you could always try curing yourself. The great thinker, Heraclitus, did this.

He fell ill with dropsy – a disease where you swell up because there's too much fluid in your body. He decided to test his doctors by asking them a riddle. 'How do you make a drought out of rainy weather?' The doctors didn't know the answer – neither do I. Do you?

So Heraclitus decided to cure himself. He reckoned the best way to get rid of too much liquid was to apply heat. In his farmyard he had a pile of rotting animal droppings – manure. The centre of the manure pile was warm.

Heraclitus buried himself up to the neck in the manure … and died.

Warning: Do *not* try this at home. If the manure doesn't kill you, your mother probably will – and your friends won't speak to you till you've had a hundred and five baths.

Perilous plague

One thing Greek doctors could do nothing about was the plague. The plague which killed hundreds in Athens in 430 BC...

• probably came from Egypt

• came so suddenly that rumours said the enemies had put poison into the water tanks

• started with a headache and sore eyes

• made breathing difficult and turned the throat red

• made victims begin to sneeze

• caused sickness when the infection moved to the stomach

- caused the temperature to rise so a plague victim couldn't stand wearing any clothes
- made victims grow terribly thirsty so they threw themselves into wells
- covered them in spots
- usually killed the victim
- often caused survivors to lose their memory:

Birds of prey wouldn't normally go near the dead bodies as they lay waiting to be buried. The birds that did always died.

The historian, Thucydides, said...

> PEOPLE DIED WHETHER THEY HAD TREATMENT OR NOT. WHAT CURED ONE PERSON OFTEN KILLED ANOTHER. SOME CAUGHT IT BY NURSING OTHERS AND THEY DIED LIKE SHEEP. IN FACT THIS WAS THE GREATEST CAUSE OF DEATH. CORPSES LAY WHERE THEY DIED ON TOP OF EACH OTHER AND THE DYING LURCHED AROUND THE STREETS AND WELLS IN THEIR CRYING NEED FOR WATER.

I FEEL SICK

MAYBE IT WAS SOMEONE YOU ATE

Some families burned their dead. Thucydides also said that passing funerals often dumped their body on somebody else's funeral fire ... then ran off!

Deadly Docs: 1

King Pyrrhus of Greece had a deadly doctor in 278 BC. The doc wrote to the Romans and said…

> DEAR FABRICUS,
> I AM THE DOCTOR TO PYRRHUS, IF YOU ARE WILLING TO PAY ME I WILL POISON THE KING

But Fabricus sent the letter straight back to Pyrrhus, his enemy, and explained…

UNTO KING PYRRHUS, GREETING,

YOU HAVE MADE A BAD CHOICE OF FRIENDS AND ENEMIES, YOU ARE AT WAR WITH HONEST MEN, BUT HAVE WICKED AND UNFAITHFUL MEN ON YOUR SIDE. AS YOU WILL SEE FROM THE LETTER THERE IS SOMEONE IN YOUR CAMP WHO PLANS TO POISON YOU. WE ARE TELLING YOU THIS BECAUSE WE DO NOT WISH TO BE BLAMED FOR SUCH A TREACHEROUS ACTION. WE WISH TO END THIS WAR HONOURABLY ON THE BATTLEFIELD.

FABRICUS

King Pyrrhus found the traitor and gave the doctor a taste of his own medicine, as it were, by having him executed. He was so grateful to the Roman enemies that he set his Roman prisoners free without a ransom.

Deadly Docs: 2

If you can't poison the enemy king then at least you can *stop* him taking medicine that would get him *better.* How? Tell him he's being poisoned by his doctor ... even if he *isn't!*

That's what Darius did to his enemy, Alexander the Great. Alexander was sick and received a letter from the double-crossing Parmenio. Like Fabricus's letter, it said...

ALEXANDER

YOUR DOCTOR, PHILIP THE ARCANIAN, HAS BEEN
PROMISED GREAT RICHES IF HE WILL POISON YOU.
BEWARE OF THE MEDICINE HE WILL GIVE YOU

PARMENIO

That evening, Doctor Philip arrived with a cup full of medicine. Alexander had the letter by his bedside. Was it really poison in the cup?

Alexander did a brave thing. He handed the letter to Doctor Philip. At the same time he drank the cup of medicine in one swallow.

Philip was impressed. 'But how do you know it wasn't poison?' he asked.

'I don't know about poison,' Alexander told him, 'but I do know about men. And I know you would never betray me, my friend.'

Alexander recovered. Not all doctors were cunning and treacherous.

Medical mystery

Which 'doctor' travelled through time to help the Greeks at Troy? (Clue: He gave them the idea about building a wooden horse.)

A WOODEN HORSE YOU SAY. THAT'S A MUCH BETTER IDEA. WE WERE GOING TO BUILD A WOODEN HEDGEHOG

Doctor Who in the 1980s British television series. (Captain Kirk of the Starship Enterprise also popped back to Troy in an episode of *Star Trek*. But Kirk decided not to interfere. Troy must have been full of time travellers and their machines. Strange that Homer didn't mention that in his poems!)

Odd Olympics

The groovy Greeks liked nothing better than a contest. The first Olympic contests were simple foot races. The first few Olympics had just one race on one day – a race of about 190 metres or the length of the stadium.

A second race – twice the length – was added in the 14th Olympics, and a still longer race was added to the 15th competition, four years later. But new events were added until the meeting lasted five days. There was even a Junior Olympics for kids.

• The bad news, girls ... females were banned from the ancient Olympics.

• The bad news, boys ... clothes were banned for the male athletes.

Choose your champion

You may wish to try an Olympic contest against the class next door. First you need to have a contest in your own class and choose your champion to represent you. Then go and cheer your champion as they compete against rival class champions.

Here's what to do. First choose your judges. They must train as judges (or referees) for ten months before the Olympics. They must also be honest. (You could have a problem finding an honest adult.) Agree the starting time and place and let the competitors battle it out.

- foot race – 200 metres
- double foot race – 400 metres
- standing long jump – with a kilo weight held in each hand to swing you through the air
- quoit-throwing (nearest to a fixed spot wins)
- javelin

After the contest...

1 Give the winners crowns made from the branches of a wild olive tree that grows in a sacred grove. (If you can't find one then make cardboard crowns from a sacred cornflakes packet.)

2 Call out the victor's name and country to the assembled crowds. (Or just phone the local newspaper.)

3 When the victor returns to their home they enter through a special gap knocked in the city wall. (Might be better if you *didn't* knock down the school wall. That's there for a purpose – to stop wild pupils escaping.)

4 The victor is treated with special favours – they either pay no taxes, or have free meals at the president's house for life. (Perhaps you could offer your victor a lifetime of free school dinners.)

5 Don't forget to cheer the loser. Losers have feelings too. (An Olympic wrestler called Timanthes lost his strength as he grew older. He was so upset he lit a big fire – then threw himself into it.)

Some groovy **Olympic** games you might not like to try

Mule-racing – smelly.

Relay – a bit hot. The god, Prometheus, stole fire from the gods and brought it down to earth for humans. But the humans had to escape from the other avenging gods. They ran with torches. The Olympic relay was run with flaming torches instead of batons, in memory of Prometheus. If the torch goes out your team loses. And if you grab the wrong end of the torch from the last runner ... ouch!

IT'S NOT MY HAND I'M WORRIED ABOUT!

Four-horse chariot race – dangerous. The poet
Homer described an accident…

EUMELOS WAS THROWN OUT OF THE
CHARIOT BESIDE THE WHEEL. THE
SKIN WAS RIPPED FROM THE ELBOWS,
NOSE AND MOUTH, AND HIS
FOREHEAD SMASHED IN OVER THE
EYEBROWS. HIS EYES FILLED WITH
TEARS AND HIS POWERFUL VOICE
WAS SILENCED.

A bit rougher than your school rounders match,
eh?

Hoplite racing – heavy, but not groovy. Wearing full armour and carrying weapons, this was hard work – try running with a couple of dustbins strapped to your back and that's how it might feel.

HOPLITE, NOT LIGHT HOP!

Trumpeters' competition – deafening.

Pancration ... what? Pancration was a bit of a mixture of boxing and wrestling. The only rule was that there were no rules, apart from no biting and no gouging out the eyes. Just flatten the opponent. You could...

- strangle
- kick
- arm-twist
- jump up and down on your opponent.

Quite good if you're a winner. Painful for a loser.

Boxing – ordinary old boxing? Yes, harmless little fisticuffs – unless you do it the ancient Greek way, as the horrible historical story of Creugas and Damoxenos shows...

The Greek Guardian
still only 20 obols
Creugas the Corpse Claims Crown

In the Olympic heavyweight championship yesterday Damoxenos, the Dark Destroyer, beat challenger Creugas... and lost the title!

In a sensational contest the two men were both defending their unbeaten records. A crowd of two thousand sat on the grass in the afternoon sunshine to enjoy a fight to the end. They didn't know what an end it was going to be.

Boos

Big Damoxenos was booed as he stepped on to the grass and had leather wrapped around his mighty fists. The handsome Creugas was cheered as he stepped forward. The voice of the referee rang out across the grassy circle.

'Remember, slaps with the open hand, punches with the fist or blows with the back of the hand are allowed. Kicking is permitted, but no head butting. Understand?'

'Yes sir,' Creugas answered boldly. Big Damoxenos just grunted.

'The fight goes on without a break until one man has had enough,' the little ref went on. 'Show you are beaten by raising your right hand in the air. Understand?'

Damoxenos just sneered. 'I'll not need to remember that,' he boasted. 'I'll not be surrendering.'

Hammer

The crowd booed again as the referee stepped back. 'Box!' he cried and Damoxenos lunged forward. He swung his fist like a mighty hammer at Creugas's head but the young man jumped back and flicked a fist at the champion's head.

That was the pattern of the fight. Big Damoxenos lumbering round, swinging huge punches but unable to catch the slippery Creugas. Just as the crowd was growing restless, the sun sank down and the referee called a halt.

'We cannot have a draw,' he cried. 'The contest will be decided by a single blow struck by each man.'

First

The crowd seemed to like that and they closed in to get a better view.

'You go first, wimp,' Damoxenos growled. The big man held his arms by his sides – the crowd held its breath.

Creugas struck a hammer blow to the champion's head. The big man just laughed. 'My turn.'

'The young man shook his head and waited for the blow that would surely knock him senseless. It didn't.

Instead the big ox hit Creugas cruelly under the ribs with straight fingers. His sharp finger nails tore through the young man's skin. He pulled back his hand and jabbed again. This time he tore out the challenger's guts.

The crowd gasped as Creugas fell lifeless to the ground.

Cheat

The ref ran forward. 'One blow is all that is allowed. You took two blows, Damoxenos, you cheat. I hereby disqualify you. I declare that Creugas is the champion!'

The crowd cheered with joy. The new champ was not available for comment.

His manager said, 'The boy done well. Deserved that win. We'll have a few drinks later to celebrate.'

Creugas will always be remembered as a champion who had guts.

Did you know...? Olympically speaking

1 There was a fine for cheating. The cheat had to pay for an expensive statue of the god Zeus. And at Olympus there were an awful lot of Zeus statues before the Greek Olympics ended. There must have been a lot of cheats.

2 The main form of cheating was to have a really good set of horses in the chariot race then have a bet that you would *lose* the race. You made sure you lost the race by pretending to whip the horses to go faster ... while secretly tugging at the reins to slow them up. This 'pulling' of horses to win money still goes on today.

3 The Greek Olympics were banned by the rotten Romans. The Romans didn't much like sport when they conquered the Greeks. The Romans preferred their own groovy 'games'… like fights to the death between gladiators … and they built huge coliseums to stage the contests. But they let the beaten Greeks keep their Olympics until miserable Roman Emperor, Theodosius, abolished them in AD 394.

4 The Greek Olympics had competitions in music, public speaking and theatre as well.

5 The Olympics vanished for 1,500 years. They were revived in 1896 by Pierre de Coubertin, a young French nobleman, and since then they have been staged every fourth year. The ancient Greek Olympics were held in honour of Zeus, and all wars would cease during the contests. The Olympics came first. Sadly, in the modern Olympics, war came first;

the games stopped during World War I and World War II (1916, 1940, 1944).

6 A cook, Coroibus of Elis, was the first recorded winner.

7 The boy athlete, Pisidorus, took his mum to the Olympics. Because women were banned, she had to be disguised as his trainer.

8 …and, talking about trainers. There are quite a few 'Nikes' at modern Olympics. But did you know that Nike was the goddess of victory, who watched over all athletic contests?

9 A sports arena was one 'stadion' (600 Olympian feet, 190 metres) long. That's why we have sports 'stadiums' today. The competitors raced up and down, not round and round.

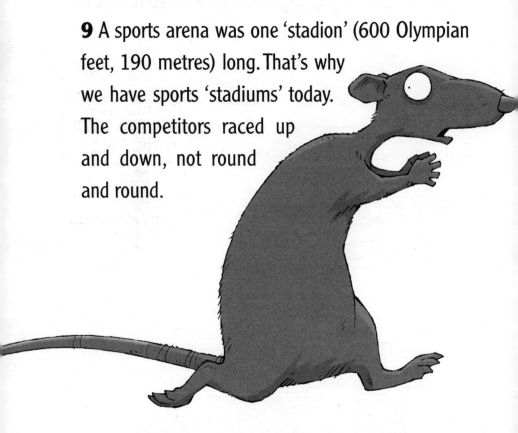

10 The poet Homer described a race between Odysseus and Achilles. Odysseus was losing and said a quick prayer to the goddess, Athene. She not only made Achilles slip – she made him fall head first into cattle droppings. He stood up spitting cow dung – and lost the race, of course.

Funny Food

Sacrificial snacks

A sacrifice is *supposed* to be a groovy gift to the gods. 'Here you are, gods, here's a present for you. I'm being nice to you, so you will be nice to me, won't you?'

When the Greeks sacrificed an animal to a god, they roasted it and they ate it. That's a bit like buying your mum a box of chocolates then scoffing them yourself.

• The greatest honour was to have some roasted heart, lungs, liver or kidney from the sacrificed animal.

• The best meat was shared around.

• Everything left was minced together and put into sausages or puddings — but the important people didn't bother with those.

• This didn't leave very much for the gods to eat, you understand. Just the tail, the thigh bones and the gall bladder.

The Greeks even mixed the blood and the fat together and stuffed it into the bladder of the animal. They then roasted and ate this little treat. Would you like to try this to see what the Greeks ate? (Without all the mess of sacrificing a cow, of course. That can make a terrible mess on the living-room carpet.) Then go to your local butcher's shop and ask for it. But what do you ask for?

1 haggis

2 black pudding

3 sausage

2 Black pudding. The Greeks roasted it while we tend to fry it in slices, but really it's the same thing.

❝DID YOU KNOW...?
VEGETARIANS IN ANCIENT GREECE
WOULDN'T SACRIFICE ANIMALS TO
THE GODS. INSTEAD THEY SACRIFICED
VEGETABLES – GROOVY, EH?❞

Munching Milon

Milon was a wrestler. He also thought he was pretty groovy. Before one Olympic contest he walked around the stadium with a live young bull on his shoulders.

He fancied a snack after all that effort, so he killed the bull and ate it. He finished the whole bull before the day was out.

But maybe there are some gods on Olympus with a sense of fair play. Because, in the end, Milon got what he deserved. *Exactly* what he deserved.

It started with him showing off again. He split open a tree with his bare hands ... but his hand became stuck in the split. Try as he might he couldn't get free. When a pack of wolves came along they licked their chops and moved in on Milon.

What did they do to Milon? Just what Milon did to the young bull – except they probably didn't cook him first.

Foul food

The Greeks ate the meat of sacrifices but didn't eat a lot of meat in their normal day-to-day lives. One historian said, 'The Greeks had meals of two courses; the first a kind of porridge – and the second a kind of porridge.'

In fact it wasn't quite that bad. The 'porridge' was more a sort of paste made up of lentils, beans and corn all ground up with oil – vegetable oil, not the sort of oil garages put in cars.

The peasants had some olives, figs, nuts or goats-milk cheese to add a bit of taste. They washed it down with water or goat's milk.

After about 500 BC the rich started to eat more meat than the peasants – goat, mutton, pork or deer – and drink wine rather than water. But what else did they eat of the following?

180

Answers

All except **3** and **7**.

Spartan soup

You might not have enjoyed living in Athens and eating grasshoppers and thrushes. But you could have been worse off. You could have lived in Sparta. The Spartans had a disgusting concoction called black broth. They mixed pork juices with salt and *vinegar* into a sort of soup.

The Athenians made some very cruel comments about Spartan food. Athenaeus said, 'The Spartans claim to be the bravest people in the world. To eat food like that they'd *have* to be.'

Another Athenian said, 'It isn't surprising the Spartans are ready to die on the battlefield – death has to be better than living on food like theirs.'

The groovy Greek guzzler

Archestratus wrote the first ever cookery book in Europe. It was written in verse and probably meant to be recited at feasts – not used as a recipe book. It contained some quirky bits of advice to eaters and to cooks. Archestratus seemed a rather grumpy man with strong views on some foods…

A PONTIC FISH, THE SAPERDE,
IS POOR AND TASTELESS AND IT SMELLS.
TO THOSE WHO EAT THIS THING I
SAY,
BOTH YOU AND IT CAN GO
TO HELL!

And Archestratus had his own favourite foods. He liked to rubbish more popular dishes...

NOW SOME MEN LIKE THE TASTE OF BEEF,
THEY SING THE PRAISES OF THE COW.
WHILE I WOULD RATHER GET MY TEETH,
INTO THE BELLY OF A SOW.

But Archestratus saved his nastiest comments for foreign cooks who ruined good Greek food with their recipes…

IF YOUR FOOD YOU WANT TO WASTE,
TAKE A BASS FISH FROM THE SEA,
FIND A COOK WITH AWFUL TASTE
LIKE THE COOKS FROM ITALY.

SYRACUSE HAS BAD COOKS TOO
SPOILING BASS IN SAUCE OF CHEESE,
OR IN PICKLES, TASTE LIKE GLUE,
KEEP AWAY FROM COOKS LIKE THESE.

Just as well he didn't live to taste our modern versions of Italian delights. He might have written a horrible verse like ...

SPAGHETTI HOOPS THAT COME IN TINS
BELONG IN DEEP AND DUSTY BINS.
AS FOR TASTELESS PLASTIC
PIZZA
SIMPLY LEAVE IT IN YOUR
FRIZZA.

Groovy Greek Growing Up

The good news: Boys didn't go to school until they were seven – girls didn't have to go to school at all.

The bad news: You didn't add up with numbers. You added up with letters – a = 1, b = 2, c = 3 and so on.

MUM'S GIVEN ME A 2-9-7 6-9-7 FOR DINNER! WONDER WHAT 4-1-4 8-1-4?

But do *you* know what number BAD + HEAD make?

Answer

$214 + 8514 = 8728$

WHAT DOES *BAD* AND *HEAD* MAKE?

A CASE FOR THE DOCTOR SIR!

The really bad news: Boys took a slave to school with them. No, *not* to do their work. The job of the slave was to make sure the boy behaved himself. If he didn't then the slave would give him a good beating.

TEST YOUR TEACHER

The Greeks loved thinking about things — the science of thinking about things became known as 'philosophy'. But it was a thinker from Italy who came up with the most curious thoughts — Zeno of Elea. The Greeks loved talking and thinking about Zeno's 'problems'. Test your teacher with this sneaky (and Greeky) question...

PLEASE, SIR, IMAGINE A RACE BETWEEN THE GREEK HERO, ACHILLES, AND A TORTOISE. ACHILLES RUNS TEN TIMES FASTER THAN THE TORTOISE; THE TORTOISE IS GIVEN A START OF TEN METRES. WILL ACHILLES EVER PASS THE TORTOISE?

HO HO HO. OF COURSE HE WILL!

WRONG! CLEVER MR ZENO OF ELEA SAID NO. EVERY TIME ACHILLES REACHES THE PLACE THE TORTOISE WAS, THE TORTOISE HAS MOVED FORWARD A TENTH OF THE DISTANCE THAT ACHILLES HAS RUN, SO THE TORTOISE WILL ALWAYS BE AHEAD

ERR... UM

Surviving school dinners

Have you ever been to school dinners and seen nothing you fancy? What happens? You go hungry.

The Lydians went hungry for a very long time because there was a famine. They decided to do something about the problem. They discovered that the more you think about food the hungrier you get. So they invented games to take their minds off food. They played dice and knucklebones.

The games were so interesting they didn't notice they were hungry. The next day they ate whatever they could find but didn't play games. This went on for 18 years! Games one day, food the next.

So, if you don't fancy a school dinner then play knucklebones. You need five ankle-joints from *cloven-footed* animals. (They make neat cubes of bone.) There are several cloven-footed animals –

bison, pigs, goats, antelopes and sheep. If any of those appear on a school-dinner menu then you might just be in luck.

If your school cook slaughters her own wildebeest in the kitchens, then ask her for the little cube-shaped bones from the ankle joint. If she *doesn't* then you'll just have to use small cubes of wood like dice.

Knucklebones: 'Horse in the Stable'

Players:

One or more players.

You need:

Five knucklebones (or wooden cubes).

Rules:

Put four knucklebones on the ground. Each one is a 'horse'.

Put the left hand near them with the fingers and thumb tips spread out and touching the ground. The gaps between the fingers are the 'stables'.

One knucklebone is tossed into the air with the right hand.

Before catching it the player must knock one 'horse' into a 'stable' with the right hand — that is, they must flick a knucklebone into a gap between the fingers.

With the right hand, catch the knucklebone that was thrown in the air.

Repeat until all four 'horses' are in their 'stables' — no more than one 'horse' to a 'stable'!

If all four are put in their 'stables' then move the left hand away from the 'horses'. Toss the throwing stone into the air with the right hand, pick up all four horses with the right hand, and catch the throwing stone in the right hand.

If the turn ends with a full 'stable', or if the player makes a mistake, pass the turn to the next person. The first to 'stable' all the 'horses' ten times is the winner!

The school Olympics

Greek children invented games like knucklebones that are still played in some parts of the world today. In fact you may even have played some of the games yourself. If you haven't, and want to play like a groovy Greek, then here are the rules for six games.

Ostrakinda

This is a game for two teams that is still played in Italy, Germany and France. You need: A silver coin. Paint one side black with poster paint – this side is 'Night'. The plain side is 'Day'.

Rules:

1 Divide into two teams – the 'Nights' and the 'Days'.

2 Spin the coin in the air.

3 If it lands black side up then the Nights chase the Days – and if it lands silver side up the Days chase the Nights.

Cooking pot

Rules:

1 Choose someone to be 'It'.

2 'It' is blindfolded and sits on the ground.

3 The others try to touch or poke 'It'.

4 'It' aims to touch one of the teasers with a foot.

5 Anyone touched by a foot becomes 'It', is blindfolded and sat on the ground.

Bronze Fly

A sort of Greek Blind-man's Buff. A Greek described it…

THEY FASTENED A HEAD–BAND ROUND A BOY'S EYES.

HE WAS THEN TURNED ROUND AND ROUND AND CALLED OUT, 'I WILL CHASE THE BRONZE FLY!'

THE OTHERS CALLED BACK, 'YOU MIGHT CHASE HIM BUT YOU WON'T CATCH HIM.'

THEY THEN TORMENT HIM WITH PAPER WHIPS UNTIL HE CATCHES ONE OF THEM.

ISN'T THAT A BULL WHIP?

Ephedrismos
Rules:

1 A player is blindfolded and gives a second one a piggy-back.

2 The rider then has to guide the player to a target set on the ground.

3 If the player succeeds then he becomes the rider. This could become a competition where pairs race to reach the target.

ARE YOU SURE THIS IS THE WAY TO THE TARGET?

Greecket

The Greeks also played ball games where you throw a ball at a 'wicket', rather like cricket without a batsman.

We just have pictures of these games that have been painted on Greek vases, but we don't have their written rules. Make up your own rules – maybe they played like this...

1 Stand on a mark a fixed distance from the wicket.

2 Take the ball and have ten attempts to hit the wicket.

3 The opponent stands behind the wicket (like a wicket-keeper) and throws the ball back to you every time.

4 Then you stand behind the wicket while your opponent has ten tries.

5 The one who has the most hits of the wicket from ten throws is the winner.

6 Try again from a different mark.

It looks (from the vase paintings) as if the loser has to give the winner a piggy-back ride.

Kottabos

Rules:

1 Take a wooden pole and stand it upright.

2 Balance a small metal disk on top of the pole.

3 Leave a little wine in the bottom of your two-handled drinking cup.

4 Grip the cup by one handle, flick the wine out and try to knock the disk off the top of the pole.

(Would you believe grown-up Greeks played this silly game at parties?)

You can try this with a cup and water and a 50p coin on the end of a broom handle ... but not in your dining-room, please.

Puzzle your parents

So your parents think they're smart, do they? Give them this simple test to check their brain-power. All they have to do is answer 'Groovy Greeks', 'Terrible Tudors' or 'Vile Victorians'…

Who had these toys or games first?
The Greeks, the Tudors or the Victorians?

1 puppets moved by strings

2 draughts

3 tug of war

4 dolls with moving parts

5 model chariots

6 yo-yos

7 babies' rattles

8 spinning-tops

9 see-saws

10 bowling hoops

Answers

All were played first by *Greek* children any other answer is wrong.

How did your parents score?

10 probably cheating

6-9 quite good – for an adult

3-5 go back to school – or read *Groovy Greeks*

0-2 never *ever* let this parent offer to help with your homework. In fact a *dead* hamster could do better.

The Romans are Coming

Bodge-up at Beneventum!

As the Greek armies grew weaker, the Romans grew stronger. At first the groovy Greeks won all the battles – but lost a lot of men each time. The Romans learned from their mistakes and got better every battle, until finally, in 275 BC...

AND WORSE WAS TO COME. A YOUNG ELEPHANT WAS MADDENED BY THE ROMAN SPEARS. IT CHARGED AROUND THE BATTLEFIELD LOOKING FOR ITS MUM. IT ALSO TRAMPLED ITS GREEK OWNERS

MUMMY!

RESULT: ROMAN 1 - GREEKS AND ELEPHANTS UNITED 0

Jumbo facts

1 The first Greek to come across an elephant army was Alexander the Great when he invaded India.

2 Apart from trampling and terrifying the enemy, elephants gave a good shooting platform for archers.

3 The Greeks used elephants supplied by India. The elephant trainers came with them. The elephants grew from babies with their trainer. No one else could command an elephant because it only understood the trainer's Indian language.

4 An elephant trainer was important to the Greeks and he was paid more than the average soldier.

5 A year after the bodge-up at Beneventum the Greeks arrived at Argos. In the battle an elephant lost its driver. The creature ran round the battlefield until it found him, dead on the ground. It picked him up with its trunk and rested the body across its tusks before carrying its dead master off the battlefield. And it wasn't too bothered who it trampled to death as it crossed the battlefield – Greek friends as well as Roman enemies.

Pathetic Pyrrhus

King Pyrrhus met a particularly pathetic end in his battle to defeat the Romans. In 274 BC he was fighting at the siege of Argos when a peasant with a pike hurt him. The peasant didn't hurt the King very much, you understand, but Pyrrhus was furious and turned to smash the pike man with his sword.

Poor Pyrrhus reckoned without the women of Argos. They had climbed up to the roof tops to watch the battle. They must have been like proud parents watching a school football match. You know, the sort who stand on the touchline and shout things like, 'Get stuck in, our Timothy!' And, 'Come on ref – get your eyes tested!'

Anyway, who should be watching Pyrrhus attacking the pike man peasant? The peasant's mum.

'Hey! That's my little boy you're trying to kill, you big bully!' she cried. The woman tore a tile off the roof and flung it at Pyrrhus.

Well, the woman was either an Olympic-standard discus thrower… or very, very lucky. The tile gave Pyrrhus a crack on the back of the neck, just below the helmet. His neck was broken and he dropped dead from his horse.

If there'd been newspapers in those days, *The Argos Chronicle* would have enjoyed that story. Imagine the headlines…

PROUD PIKE PEASANT'S PARENT POTS PATHETIC PYRRHUS

… perhaps?

Epilogue

After the groovy Greeks came the rotten Romans. The Romans were supposed to be an even greater people than the Greeks. After all, they eventually ruled over half the world — including Britain.

But the Romans were pretty rotten compared to the Greeks. Their games weren't great sports events like the Olympics — they were just an excuse to watch humans kill animals, animals kill humans, animals kill animals and humans kill humans. In boxing, for example, the Greeks bound their hands with leather bands like boxing gloves. The Romans bound their hands with leather bands — but put vicious spikes in them.

The Greek plays had been exciting and interesting. The Romans tried to copy them but were looking for more action and violence. Roman plays eventually killed people on stage for real.

One story about the take-over of Greece by the Romans gives a good example of what the world lost when the rotten Romans took over from the groovy Greeks...

Archimedes was a brilliantly clever Greek. When the Romans attacked his people in the city of Syracuse (211 BC) Archimedes used his great and groovy brain to invent wonderful new weapons.

For two years the Romans were kept out of the city as the inventor created 'death-rays' – giant mirrors that reflected the sun on to Roman ships in the harbour and set them on fire – and huge catapults that drove them off.

But at last the Romans broke through the Greek defences and brought terror to the citizens of Syracuse as they killed and stole from the houses. The Roman commander had given one strict order, however: 'Find Archimedes – but don't hurt the great man.'

At last a Roman soldier burst into Archimedes' house. The inventor was in the middle of an experiment and was too busy to bother with a small matter like an invasion at that moment.

The Roman was puzzled. Why was this old man ignoring him?

The Roman became angry. How *dare* this old man ignore him?

The Roman lost his cool. He killed the

defenceless inventor. With one blow he destroyed one of the cleverest men the world has known.

The Roman soldier was punished for disobeying the commander's order not to harm Archimedes. But that didn't bring the old man back. Just as none of even the greatest Roman achievements could bring back the glory of the Greeks.

The rotten Romans ruled – the groovy Greeks went to their graves. That's horrible history for you.

GROOVY GREEKS

Quiz

Gruesome Greek quiz

Simply answer 'Yea' for yes or 'Nay' for no to these facts about the grisly Greeks.

1 In the story of Troy, King Agamemnon sacrifices his daughter to the gods. Would that have really happened in ancient Greece?

2 A slave called Aesop told great stories such as 'The Tortoise and the Hare'. He was richly rewarded by the Greek priests.

3 The people who lived in the city of Sparta were super-tough kids. One Spartan boy hid a stolen fox cub under his tunic and didn't let on, even though the fox ate the boy's guts away.

4 In Draco's Athens (c. 600 BC) the laws were strict and you could be whipped for stealing a cabbage.

5 Athens' ruler Peisistratus (605–527 BC) arranged to have himself attacked so the people would feel sorry for him.

6 Teacher Socrates taught his students not to believe in the old Greek gods. Socrates was hanged.

7 General Alcibiades (450–404 BC) wanted people to notice him. Once he cut off his dog's tail to get a bit of attention.

8 The Greeks read the future using the guts of dead birds.

9 Hecate was the Greek goddess of crossroads. Greeks left food at crossroads for her.

10 The Greeks painted the doors of their houses red with blood.

Suffering Spartans

The Spartans were the toughest of all the Greek peoples – and it was extra-tough for Spartan kids.

Here's a Spartan rule book with some of the words missing. Get the answers right – or take a savage Spartan punishment!

The missing words, in the wrong order, are: **no clothes, hair, herd, thistles, mountains, whipped, baths, girls, bite, beaten.**

1 A bad serving-child will receive a _____ on the back of the hand.

2 A sickly baby will be taken to the _____.

3 A new bride must cut off her _____ and dress like a man.

4 Children caught stealing food will be _____.

5 A child belongs to the state of Sparta. At the age of seven children will join a _____.

6 A Spartan child may have only a few _____ a year.

7 In processions, dances and temple services girls must wear _____.

8 If a Spartan child is cold in winter, then they may sleep under _____.

9 Good Spartans are _____ at the altar of the goddess Artemis.

10 _____ are to be trained for fitness by running, wrestling, and throwing quoits and javelins.

Test your teacher quiz

Everyone studies the Greeks at school. Greek history lessons were even around when your teachers went to school, so they should know the answers to these ten quick questions.

1 General Alcibiades hated the Greek gods and damaged their statues. He smashed off what part of the statues? (Clue: he only did this to the male gods)

2 The superstitious Greeks did not like dreaming of seeing your own face in a mirror. What did they think you would do soon after? (Clue: never see your face in a mirror again!)

3 Around 375 BC the girls of Attica went to the local temple and ran round the woods pretending to be bears. What did they wear? (Clue: don't try this at the North Pole)

THEY'RE ALL BEAR!

4 Greek teacher Aristotle had a favourite food that you will probably never eat. What? (Clue: unless you are stranded in the Sahara desert)

5 Playwright Aeschylus died (it is said) when an eagle dropped an animal on his head. What? (Clue: a slow death?)

6 Greek teacher Gorgias was born in a strange place. In his mother's what? (Clue: he was dead lucky to be alive, but Mum wasn't.)

7 Greeks invented a nasty weapon. It was a liquid that caught fire as soon as it landed and set fire to everything it touched in open air. What was it called? (Clue: not Roman water but…)

8 Aesculapius was a Greek doctor. Some of his cures worked. Some of the stories of other cures are plain daft. How did he cure (they say) water on a girl's brain? (Clue: she got it in the neck)

9 Doctor Hippocrates practised cutting out a circle of the skull to drain fluids off the brain. But why did the patient take home the circle of bone? (Clue: like a rabbit's foot?)

10 Some vegetarian Greeks refused to sacrifice animals to the gods. What did they sacrifice instead? (Clue: obvious really!)

Answers

Gruesome Greek quiz

1 Yea. At the time of the Trojan Wars, not only were children sacrificed but bits of them were eaten too. Aren't you glad you weren't around?

2 Nay. In fact they took him to the top of a cliff and threw him off. It seems a few of his stories upset them.

3 Yea. This was a popular story told by the Spartans. Of course it may have just been Spartan boasting and a big fib. But it's a warning – don't go sticking foxes (or bears or budgies) up your jumper!

4 Nay. Draco was much tougher than that! The punishment for pinching an apple or a cabbage was death! By the way, the punishment for idleness was also death! (Think of all those dead teachers in your school if we still had that law!)

5 Yea. Peisistratus staggered into Athens bruised and bleeding and said the city would suffer if its people didn't protect him. But he had arranged the attack on himself. The people of Athens were tricked into protecting him ... even though they hated him.

6 Nay. He was sentenced to death by poisoning. And he had to drink the poison himself. Which he did. So he carried out his own death sentence. Why not ask your teacher to demonstrate how a brave teacher behaves?

7 Yea. Alcibiades was a pretty good Athenian general but switched sides to the Spartan enemies. But the Spartans didn't trust the traitor much. In the end he was murdered, shot full of Spartan arrows, and his dog would have wagged its tail in joy – if Alcibiades hadn't cut it off, that is.

8 Yea. Don't try this at home with your pet parrot. You'll make a right mess on the carpet. Stick to reading horoscopes in the newspaper.

9 Yea. She always had a pack of howling dogs with her. (If you want to carry on this ancient Greek habit then why not leave a tin of dog food at your nearest crossroads, eh? Seems a shame for Hecate to get all the grub.)

10 Nay. They painted them black with tar! They believed evil spirits would stick to the tar and be kept out. Messy.

Suffering Spartans

1 Bite. Younger boys had to serve older boys. If the younger boy did something wrong he could be given a nasty nip!

2 Mountains. Babies were left up a mountain to die if they failed a health check.

3 Hair. And a bridegroom had to pretend to carry his bride off by force.

4 Beaten. Children were kept hungry and encouraged to steal food! (Spartans thought sneakiness was a handy skill in battle.) If the kids were caught stealing, they'd be beaten for being careless enough to get caught!

5 Herd. The toughest child was allowed to become leader and order the others about.

6 Baths. Stinky Spartans!

7 No clothes. So they didn't get fancy ideas about fine clothes.

8 Thistles. Children slept on beds of rushes that they gathered themselves from the river bank. In winter they could mix a few thistles in with the reeds – the prickles were supposed to give them a feeling of warmth!

9 Whipped. A horribly historical way to prove you were a good Spartan! The one who suffered the most lashes was the toughest. Some bled to death.

10 Girls. So don't mess with a Spartan miss.

Test your teacher quiz

1 Their naughty bits. Alcibiades knocked off the naughty bits on the statues of the naked gods. Ouch!

2 Die. Mind you, some people are so hideous they'd

probably die if they saw themselves in a mirror awake! (Bet you know people like that!)

3 Nothing. This was supposed to prepare them for being grown women. The crazy chases were supposed to get the last wild bits of fun out of them before they became boring adults.

4 Camel. Maybe we should start serving camel at posh tea parties. You turn to your guest and say, 'One hump or two?'

5 A tortoise. We do not know how the tortoise was after the accident. If it lived it was probably a bit shell-shocked though.

6 Coffin. Gorgias's mother died and was popped in a coffin but somehow the baby was born anyway. He grew up and taught his students, 'Nothing exists – not even me!' If I'd been his student I'd have just skived off school then!

7 Greek Fire. Even today no one is sure how Greek Fire was made. But it was nasty stuff. Not the sort of thing you'd want to spray on your barbecue.

8 He cut off her head. After the water drained off he sewed the head back on. Hummmm! Believe that and you are ready for a new head yourself!

9 For luck. The superstitious Greeks kept the bone as a good-luck charm. It was supposed to keep you safe from disease.

10 Vegetables. They killed carrots, cracked corn and carved cabbages cruelly and then they probably battered some poor beans brutally. Vile vegetarians, how could they?

Interesting Index

fire, stealing 163
flames, throwing 84, 133
food, foul 42–3, 174–85
foxes 47–9, 218, 226

games, good 191–206
ghosts 55, 77, 86, 90, 104
girls 127, 220, 222
    Attican 126, 223
    banned 158
    growing up 186
    Spartan 40, 231
gold 10
Gordian knot, unfastened 89
Gorgias (Greek teacher) 131, 136, 224, 233
grasshoppers, eating 180–1
Greek fire 134, 136, 233
greeket (good game) 200–1
guts 105, 168, 218–19

Hecate (Greek goddess) 104, 220, 228
hemlock (putrid poison) 64–7
Heraclitus (Greek philosopher) 148
Herodotus (Greek historian) 44, 73, 75
Hestia (Greek goddess) 125
Hippocrates (Greek doctor)

140–2, 144–7, 225
historians, horrible 32, 44, 73, 85, 115, 151, 179
Homer (Greek poet) 9, 86, 156, 164, 173
hoplite racing 165
horses 169
    wooden 17–20, 25, 34–5, 156

idleness 57, 227

judges, honest 160

keres (wicked spirits) 106
knucklebones (good game) 191–5
kottabos (good game) 202–3

laws, lousy 56–9, 67, 122–3, 219, 227
Leonidas, (Spartan king) 49
Lydians, hungry 191

madness 104
magicians 55
manure (rotten droppings) 148–9
Marathon, battle of 11, 70
Milon (Greek wrestler) 178–9